Suzie the Baker

By Sonya Connor

Illustrated by TullipStudio

Suzie The Baker

This is a work of fiction. Names, characters, places, and incidents either are the product of the author's imagination or are used fictitiously. Any resemblance to actual persons, living or dead, events, or locales is entirely coincidental.

Copyright © 2023 by Sonya Connor

All rights reserved. No part of this book may be reproduced or used in any manner without written permission of the copyright owner except for the use of quotations in a book review. For more information: sunshinereadingadventures.com.

First Hardcover edition August 2023

ISBN 978-1-961649-05-7 (Hardcover)
Library of Congress Control Number: 2023910126

www.sunshinereadingadventures.com

Suzie's class would like to take a field trip.
But they will need to get some funds for it.
The teacher suggests that they have a bake sale.
They decide on a goal, they must not fail!

Suzie tells mom about the sale, she is eager.
But Mom does not know how to bake either.
They decide they will do some practice runs.
Before turning in their baked goods buns.

They search online for some yummy recipes.
They look for some they could bake with ease.
Shopping list in hand, they head to the store.
They decide that they will try a total of four.

First they will try chocolate chip cookies.
A plate of cookies will be sure to please.
The recipe says 15 minutes bake time.
Suzie is thinking, "I can't wait to taste mine!"

Suzie turns up the temperature knob.
Thinking that she was doing a great job.
What's that smell? It's cookies burning!
Suzie tells mom that it was her doing.

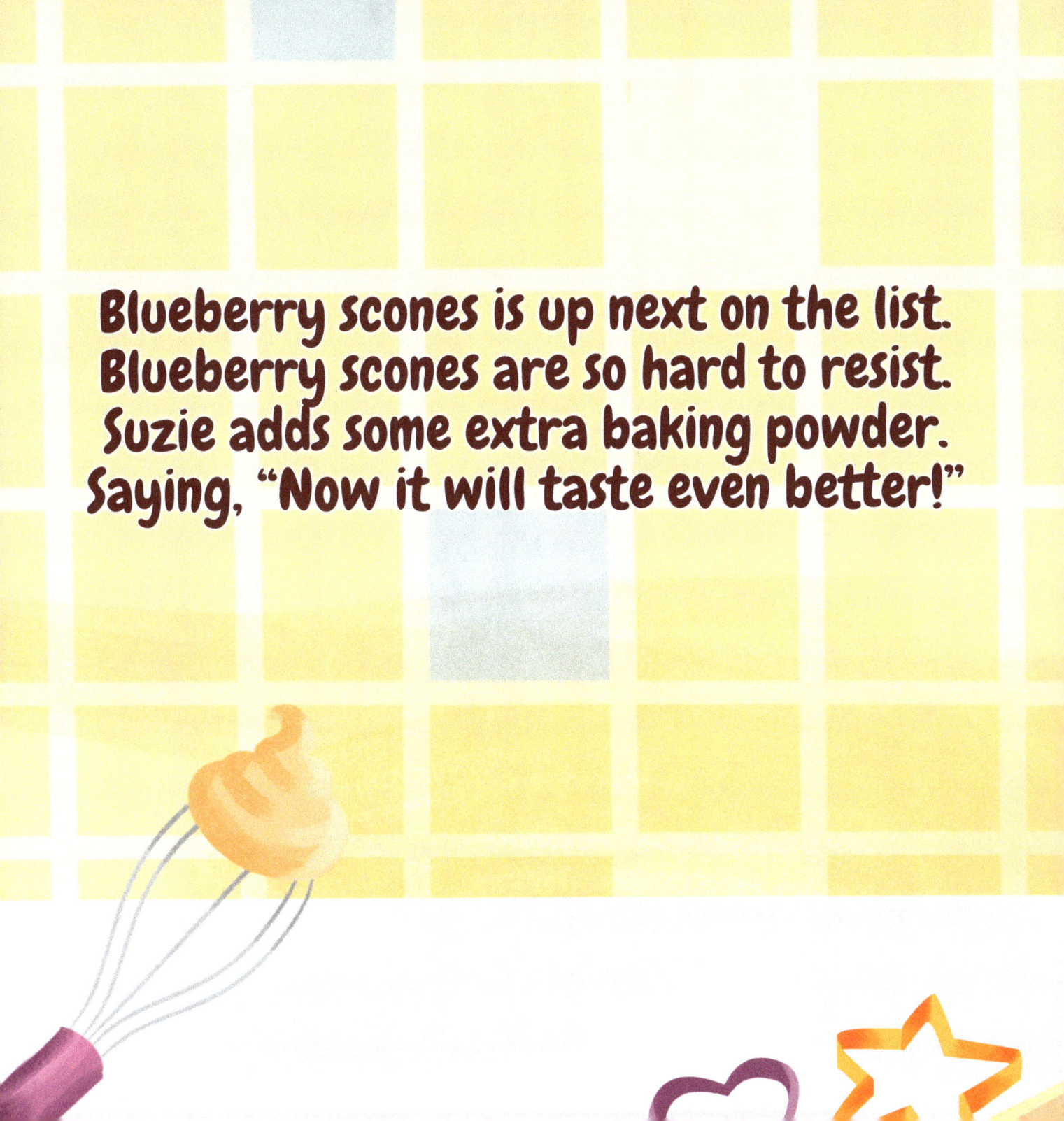

Blueberry scones is up next on the list.
Blueberry scones are so hard to resist.
Suzie adds some extra baking powder.
Saying, "Now it will taste even better!"

The scones go in the oven, they take a break.
Thinking about delicious layers of scone flake.
Then KA-POW! The oven door flies open.
Scone mix spills out from where it had risen.

Time for the apple pie easy peasy recipe.
Warm apple pie always smells heavenly.
Suzie peels the apples; the crust is next up.
She scoops up some salt with the measuring cup.

She watches the apple pie bubbling as it bakes.
She's ready to try it, gets out some plates.
She takes a bite, expecting a delicious taste.
But the saltiness shows in Suzie's surprised face.

Time to get out the electric cake mixer.
Cakes are always a good crowd pleaser.
They now carefully follow the cake recipe.
Mom says, "This will turn out splendidly!"

They double check all of the ingredients.
Mom and Suzie now have full confidence.
Suzie turns on the mixer without the cover on.
Cake batter goes flying; it's now all gone.

Mom tells Suzie, "We can go back to the store,"
"They sell cookies, scones, pies, cakes, and more!"
Suzie replies to mom, "We must not give up!"
"I found out that we can make muffins in a cup!"

They line up some mugs, add the dry items and stir.
They stir in the liquid items very carefully now.
The muffins cook up quickly in the microwave.
Suzie hopes the muffins will be the bake sale save.

The muffins turn out great, it's a high five.
Time to pack them up for the short school drive.
Suzie adds the muffins to the baked goods table.
Teacher then adds the mug muffins label.

The baked goods sale is a successful event.
Suzie tells mom about how great it all went.
She says, "Mom, let's go back to the store!"
"I now want to bake brownies, bread and more!"

Printed in the USA
CPSIA information can be obtained
at www.ICGtesting.com
LVHW081932271023
762372LV00008B/476